INVESTING IN MONEY TRADING

A Guild peak to trade currency
with financial gain

All rights reserved. No part of this publication may be reproduced, distributed, or transmitted in any form or by any means, including photocopying, recording, or other electronic or mechanical methods, without the prior written permission of the publisher, except in the case of brief quotations embodied in critical reviews and certain other noncommercial uses permitted by copyright law.

Copyright © Lawrence O. 2022.

TABLE OF CONTENT

Chapter 1

CURRENCY TRADING

Chapter 2

CURRENCY MOVEMENT

Chapter 3

CRUCIAL VERSUS SPECIALIZED EXAMINATION

Chapter 4

RISK THE BOARD PROCEDURES

FORWARD

Investing in money trading can be a very bankable strategy of earning payment income possible by utilizing your smart device. Nevertheless, the risks involved are comparatively huge. Get all the guide you need here in other for you to attain the peak in trading

Chapter 1:

Currency Trading

Exchanging any venture market is undeniably challenging as proven by the way that most starting merchants lose cash. Be that as it may, achievements can be found with enough of the right schooling, practice, and experience. Anyway, what is cash exchanging, and is it appropriate for you?

Previously, cash exchange was principally done by banks, institutional financial backers, and flexible investments. In any case, on account of advances in innovation, in a real sense, anybody can exchange monetary forms today.

Cash exchanging happens on the unfamiliar trade market - a worldwide commercial center wherein brokers all around the world exchange monetary standards. This market is the biggest monetary market on the planet, with around $5 trillion in monetary standards exchanged consistently

The unfamiliar trade market is an overall commercial center where vendors from everywhere in the world trade monetary standards. With a day-to-day cash exchange of $5 trillion, this market is the biggest monetary market on the planet.

What is Currency Trading

A cash exchanging stage is a product interface given by money specialists to their clients to give them access as dealers in the forex markets

How Does Currency Trading Work

Cash exchange is a 24-hour market that is just shut from Friday night to Sunday night, however, the 24-hour exchanging meetings are misdirected. Three meetings incorporate the European, Asian, and United States exchanging meetings.

How money exchanging works is somewhat basic. At the point when you exchange monetary standards, you're wagering on the worth of one money compared with another.

What Moves Currencies

A rising measure of stock dealers is looking into the money markets because large numbers of the powers that move the financial exchange likewise move the cash market. One of the biggest is the organic market. At the point when the world needs more dollars, the worth of the dollar increments, and when there are excesses of circling the cost drops.

Different variables like loan costs, new financial information from the biggest nations, and international pressures are only a couple of the occasions that might influence money costs.

Who Invented Currency Trading

The trading of unfamiliar monetary standards returns to early human development and the approach of shipping lanes and business. Nonetheless, current forex exchanging started in 1973, when the best quality level of unfamiliar trade was deserted and free-drifting monetary forms were taken on.

The 10 most exchanged monetary standards in the world

1. Money .   Symbol
2. US Dollar.   USD
3. Euro .   EUR
4. Japanese.   Yen JPY
5. Pound Sterling .   GBP
6. Australian Dollar. AUD
7. Canadian Dollar.   CAD
8. Swiss Franc .   CHF
9. Chinese Renminbi . CNH
10. Hong Kong Dollar . HKD
11. New Zealand Dollar . NZD

Regardless of whether you have never effectively exchanged monetary forms, you've presumably had some experience trading monetary forms. For instance, on the off chance that you've taken an occasion abroad, you no doubt traded your home money for global cash. By trading one cash for another, you took part in an unfamiliar trade market.

The Advantages of Cash Exchanging

Low Capital Prerequisites

One of the fundamental attractions of cash exchange is that you don't have to have a large chunk of change, to begin with. This implies that few financial backers can undoubtedly enter the market.

A little store can go quite far

The explanation you needn't bother with a ton of cash flow to begin exchanging monetary forms is that it's feasible to utilize 'influence' to control a lot of cash with only a little store. How influence works is that you acquire cash from your merchant to exchange with more cash than you have kept in your record.

Exchange costs are low

One more advantage of cash exchange is that exchange costs are low. Ordinarily, there are no exchange charges on cash exchanges. The fundamental type of expense that brokers pay is the spread between the purchase and the selling cost of the exchange (erring on this later).

You can exchange at whatever point you like

Finally, one more huge benefit of cash exchange is that you can exchange on your timetable. The unfamiliar trade market is open 24 hours every day, five days per week. Exchanging starts with the launch of the Sydney meeting on Monday morning and closes with the New

York meeting on Friday night, and that implies there's a lot of chance to exchange.

Why Traders Trade the Major Pairs

The volume will in general draw in more volume. This is because with more volume, spreads between the bid and ask value will generally be restricted. The significant matches have bunches of volume. They accordingly will generally have more modest spreads than intriguing matches and draw in the most dealers to them, which keeps the volume high. High volume likewise implies that merchants can enter and leave the market effortlessly, with enormous position sizes. In lower volume matches it could be more challenging to sell or purchase an enormous situation without making the cost move essentially.

High volume implies more individuals able to trade at a given time, as well, bringing about a more modest possibility of slippage, or more modest slippage when it happens. Saying this doesn't imply that enormous slippage can't occur in significant matches. It can, albeit considerably less so than in meagerly exchanged fascinating matches.

How Are Prices of the Major Pairs Determined

The monetary forms of the significant matches are free-drifting, meaning their still up in the air by the organic market. National banks might step in to control the cost, however regularly just when it is important to keep the cost from rising or falling so much that it could hurt.

Organic markets are impacted by monetary or central circumstances in every nation, financing costs, future assumptions for the nation/cash, and current positions — places that should be left sooner or later.

Going long or short

Whenever you have picked the cash pair that you need to exchange, the subsequent stage is to conclude whether the base money will fortify or debilitate against the counter money, and take a position in like manner.

Assuming you accept that the base money will fortify against the counter cash, you purchase (or 'go long') the cash pair. Assuming you believe that the base money will debilitate against the counter cash, you sell (or 'go short') the cash pair.

So for instance, assuming you accept that the British Pound will reinforce against the US Dollar, you purchase GBP/USD. On the other hand, if you figure the British Pound will weaken against the US Dollar, you sell GBP/USD.

Benefit and misfortune

Your benefit or misfortune will rely upon the degree to which you get your expectation right.

In money exchanging, benefits are estimated in 'pips.' A pip is the littlest move cash can make. In a money pair that is evaluated to four decimal places like GBP/USD, a pip is a valuable development of 0.0001. Assuming you purchase GBP/USD at 1.2500 and close the exchange at 1.2510, your benefit is 10 pips.

The financial worth of your benefit or misfortune will rely heavily on how much cash was taken on the exchange and how much influence was utilized.

Chapter 2:

Currency Movement

What drives Currency Movement

A money's solidarity is impacted by market interest elements. On the off chance that interest for money expands, it's worth will rise. Be that as it may, assuming that request diminishes, it's worth will fall.

Various elements can impact market interest for cash. Here is a glance at a portion of the primary elements:

Loan fees

A nation's loan fees significantly affect market interest for its money. If a nation expands its loan costs, interest for its money will in general increment as unfamiliar capital streams into the country. Nonetheless, if a nation brings down its loan costs, interest for its cash will in general fall as unfamiliar capital streams out of the country.

Expansion

A nation's pace of expansion (the delicate expansion in the costs of labor and products over the long run) can likewise affect the organic market for its money. A high expansion rate can prompt decreased requests.

Financial execution

Nations that are major areas of strength monetarily see the expanded interest for their monetary standards. On the other hand, nations that are encountering monetary difficulties will quite often see diminished interest in their monetary standards.

A few monetary markers that cash dealers frequently screen include:

Gross Domestic Product (GDP)

This is a wide proportion of the general strength of an economy.

The joblessness rate: joblessness influences customer spending which, thus, influences financial development.

Retail deals information: customer utilization represents the biggest piece of a nation's GDP so deals information can give important knowledge about the well-being of an economy.

Opinion reviews: feeling studies like buying supervisors' files (PMIs) can give an understanding of a nation's degree of monetary development or compression.

Obligation

A country's obligation levels can likewise affect interest for its cash. Nations with huge obligations corresponding to their GDP will more often than not be less appealing to unfamiliar financial backers. This means lower interest for their monetary standards.

Political steadiness

Unfamiliar financial backers will quite often search out politically-stable nations while money management their capital. Political unrest in a nation can bring about lower interest for its money as unfamiliar capital moves to additional steady nations.

Chapter 3:

Crucial Versus Specialized Examination

The crucial investigation includes taking a gander at all suitable data that could influence a money's solidarity or shortcoming. Here of examination, merchants take a gander at financial factors, for example, loan fees, expansion, and joblessness information to decide if money will rise or fall.

The specialized investigation, then again, includes dissecting value diagrams and pointers to foresee a cash's future developments. Here of investigation, merchants center around diagram examples and patterns and utilize authentic value developments to foresee future cost developments.

3 well known specialized examination procedures

- ***Pattern exchanging:*** the technique intends to catch gains by dissecting a cash's pattern. A pattern happens when money moves in a single heading for a significant period. Whenever you have distinguished the pattern, it could be feasible to benefit from it by exchanging a similar course as the pattern.

- ***Backing and obstruction exchanging:*** This system plans to catch gains by recognizing money's help and opposition levels. Support is the level where the cash cost finds it hard to fall beneath. Opposition is the level where the cash cost finds it challenging to go above. When these regions have been distinguished, it could be feasible to benefit by putting exchanges in the region where the money's cost is probably going to switch.

- ***Breakout exchanging:*** This methodology intends to catch gains by distinguishing monetary standards that have gotten through laid-out help or obstruction levels. Breakouts can be areas of strength for me, particularly when affirmed by other specialized examination pointers.

Fostering a bunch of exchanging rules

After you have figured out which type of examination you will use to exchange monetary standards, the subsequent stage is to foster a strong arrangement of exchanging rules. This will assist you with keeping up with the discipline and diminish risk.

This piece of your procedure ought to zero in on:

The position estimating:

Determining your ideal position size is a significant piece of an exchanging technique.

The section focuses: Your arrangement ought to consist of decisions that decide when to enter a long or short situation in a given cash pair.

Leave focuses:

Your arrangement ought to likewise have decisions that decide when to leave a long or short position.

Stop misfortune:

An exchanging plan ought to likewise zero in on risk the board devices like stop misfortunes.

There is no single equation for progress concerning exchanging monetary standards. The key is, to begin with, a fundamental technique and refine it over the long run.

Dangers of cash exchanging:

Any type of effective money management or exchange implies dangers and cash exchange is the same.

Chapter 4:

Risk The Board Procedures

Two principal dangers to know with money exchanging

Instability risk:

The unfamiliar trade market can be profoundly unstable. While this instability can set out exchanging open doors, it can likewise be a gamble factor. Startling news can altogether affect money values and horrible value developments can bring about huge misfortunes for dealers. If you don't have adequate assets in your exchanging record to cover likely misfortunes, your positions might be shut down consequently.

Influence risk:

While influence is an amazing asset that can amplify gains, it can likewise amplify misfortunes. On the off chance that a lot of influence is utilized to exchange, even a moderately little cost development of course can bring about significant misfortunes. It's essential to know that misfortunes can surpass the sum contributed.

You can never dispose of hazard totally while exchanging monetary forms, be that as it may, you can lessen it by zeroing in on risk on the board.

Two key systems that can assist with diminishing gambling include
- *Deciding your ideal position size:* before you begin exchanging monetary standards, you ought to decide your ideal position size for each exchange. A decent guideline is to try not to

gamble over 2% of your capital on any single exchange. Exchanging over 2% per exchange could open you to misfortunes that are difficult to recuperate from.

- **_Setting up stop misfortunes:_** stop misfortunes are an essential part of a strong gamble in the executive's methodology. Stop misfortunes assist with limiting exchanging misfortunes by finishing off losing positions before huge misfortunes develop.

Normal errors amateur merchants make

Exchanging without a technique

Before putting an exchange, fostering a strategy is significant. This ought to frame how you will enter and exit both winning and losing exchanges. If you don't have an exchange procedure, you are expanding your gamble.

Disregarding risk the executives

Risk the board is one of the most central pieces of a fruitful exchanging methodology. Instruments, for example, stop misfortunes and assist with limiting huge misfortunes. Having a stop misfortune for each exchange is a reasonable move.

Gambling a lot of cash in an exchange

Numerous fledgling cash dealers risk beyond what they can bear because they don't comprehend the nuts and bolts of position measuring and influence. By finding out about these ideas, you'll decrease the gamble of losing more capital than you wanted to.

Permitting feelings to direct an exchanging methodology

Misfortunes never feel better. In any case, they are essential for cash exchange. No merchant makes an ideal exchange like clockwork. The key is to acknowledge that misfortunes are an ordinary piece of exchange and adhere to your arrangement on the off chance that you experience misfortune. Try not to allow feelings to direct your exchanging methodology.